To get all the resources you'll need to help you apply the wisdom in this book to you, your family, or your team, go to www.linktr.ee/BistroBook

"Everyone needs a 'Bob' in their life! This quick assembly of short stories is a great way to learn some fast lessons that will improve your life. *At the Bistro with Bob* is an easy way to advance your character development and see opportunities to improve your legacy. I'd highly recommend to anyone that they sit and enjoy some time at The Bistro with Bob."

—Danny Silk, author of *The Way of the Dragon Slayer* and *Keep Your Love On!*

"This book is an invitation to listen in to a conversation between close friends about the most important issues in life. Filled with profound insights on family, faith, and finances, their story invites you to consider your own—and perhaps embrace a little more joy, live with an abundance mindset, and step forward with courage. A true gift to join Bob and Eric at The Bistro!"

—Peter Greer, president and CEO of HOPE International

"I forgot I was reading a book because it felt like Eric and Bob just scooted over in their booth to make room for me to join them. Accepting their invitation might be the best decision I've made in a long time. Authentic, gritty, heartfelt, and sincere, these are the stories of two men who often broke bread together but, even more, broached the most important pieces of life with intention and vulnerability. Each short chapter uncovers just a bit more of that part deep down inside each of us that wants more but doesn't always know how to ask for it. Thank you, Eric, for sharing Bob with us. He is so much of what the world needs more of right now. And, yes, I'll take a glass of wine even if I am headed back to work later. Cheers to long lunches and lives of purpose."

—Chris Field, founder of Mercy Project and author of *Disrupting for Good*

"Eric Dunavant is an intentional man and has written a beautiful story about his interactions with his mentor. As you read the timeless truths about common sense, celebration, and joy, you will be moved to pray for your own Bob Prichard to come into your life. Following the Lord is not always an easy path, but He has plans to give you hope and a future."

—Bob Hasson, CEO of HPCI; author of *Shortcuts* and coauthor of *Wired to Hear* with Shawn Bolz and *The Business of Honor* with Danny Silk; and cohost of the *Exploring the Marketplace* podcast with Shawn Bolz

"Seldom have I ever seen anyone come to life from the page as vividly as Bob Prichard of New Orleans in this remarkable short volume by Eric Dunavant. I literally couldn't put it down. And by the end, I was uplifted, inspired, and encouraged. What a man!

I am truly eager to see Eric's next literary effort because I got so much value out of this one."

—Rabbi Daniel Lapin, author of *The Holistic You*

"Eric Dunavant's new book, *At the Bistro with Bob*, is a testament to godly mentorship in a time of famine for young men starved of such opportunities. Along the way it also manages to be a manifesto for the true ROI—return on intention—and for good, practical counsel on the importance of the basics, such as dividends in investment selection and the avoidance of the overpriced, unneeded complexity that comes out of giant Wall Street investment firms. It is a celebration of the simplicity that comes from discarding the extraneous and reinvesting your freed-up time and attention on a short list of things that really deserve them. So many young men never get what they need from their fathers, uncles, or employers. This is a chance to join Eric in sitting down with Bob and getting some wisdom you may have missed earlier in life. Think of it like *Rich Dad Poor Dad* but with more riches than just money."

—Jerry Bowyer, president of Bowyer Research

"As someone who has coached Eric and witnessed his relentless work ethic firsthand, I can attest that this book reflects the same attention to detail and commitment to excellence that he brings to everything he does. In a world obsessed with financial returns, Eric gives us something far more valuable: a master class in 'return on intention.' Through the lens of his profound friendship with Bob Prichard, Eric shows us how intentional relationships, uncommon sense, and the pursuit of joy create true abundance.

What makes this book special isn't just the wisdom within its pages; it's also that Eric lives these principles daily. I've watched him transform complex financial concepts into simple, actionable strategies that serve families for generations. His dedication to understanding and implementing Bob's teachings mirrors the same intensity I've seen him bring to his own growth and development.

This isn't just another business book. It's a road map for building a legacy that will bless generations. Anyone seeking to align their wealth with what matters most will find wisdom and inspiration in these pages. Additionally, the Prichard Principles aren't just ideas; they're transformative truths that Eric has tested and proven in both his personal life and professional practice. He's given us a gift: the kind of wisdom that comes only from a mentor who truly understands that relationships trump returns."

—Josiah Novak, founder and CEO of
The True Transformation

"Before reading this book, I used to 'set goals' and 'leverage relationships,' and wow, did I have it all wrong. With Eric's guidance, I've learned to be more intentional about what I go after as well as how to build relationships instead of 'use them.' That's not just a subtle shift in words—it's a better way to get important things done: to grow business faster, deliver more value, and increase my investment capital. How does this book move such big rocks? Eric's writing dropped me right into important business conversations that feel very familiar to me—conversations we've all had before at one level or another—but the insights he draws from these conversations are extraordinary. With each new chapter, I hit my forehead, thinking, *Why hadn't I thought of that angle or perspective?* Well, there's a reason I hadn't thought of that—Eric's mind is built differently than most. Dive in and see the kind of results someone with unshakeable faith can create, and find ways to strengthen your own faith and tap into your untouched potential."

—Oren Klaff, founder and managing director at
Intersection Capital

At the Bistro with Bob

At the Bistro with Bob

*Learning to Pursue Joy,
Celebrate Relationships, and
Use Common Sense*

ERIC L. DUNAVANT

This book is dedicated to my amazing wife, Angel. She is my greatest editor, copywriter, and ghost writer. Every time I was stuck, she would remind me of a story or event we experienced with Bob and Raydene, and I found the path to keep writing.

To Clayton, Austen, and Gracyn: You've taught me so much about myself. Being your father is the greatest gift I've ever received. Watching you grow from children into young adults is a blessing. I am excited to watch as we grow our own family story together.

To Darcy and "Tiger": Thank you for sharing Bob. Thank you for sharing the stories of your dad and grandpa after he was gone. We all miss him, and I hope that this book will create a path to share Bob and his love for life with the rest of the world.

To Collin, Andy, and the 5 a.m. crew at Anytime Fitness: Thank you for asking me questions and pushing me to finish this book. Your encouragement made it possible for me to stay the course and cross the finish line of this storytelling journey.

To the men of Syndicate: Thank you for challenging me to be a better man. Iron sharpens iron, and your collective friendship has forced me to look in the mirror every morning and ask if I like what I see.

Table of Contents

Introduction

This book is inspired by a true story. Bob Prichard was an extraordinary man and a dear friend. For more than a decade, I had the privilege of sharing lunch with Bob once or twice a month. Throughout our friendship, the stories he shared were like stepping stones—leading me to a more intentional and abundant life.

In the following chapters, Bob represents not only himself but also the many remarkable mentors who have shaped my life and influenced my journey. While the stories about Bob in this book are based on actual events—either ones Bob told me personally or ones that were relayed to me through his daughter and grandson after he passed—they carry a deeper meaning.

My son Austen once reflected on one of his favorite books, saying, "This story is grounded in truth, but it may not always follow the exact details." I followed that strategy as I condensed over a decade of interactions with Bob Prichard into a handful of years recorded in this book. The essence of what follows is true, but the compression forced me to change some details, timelines, and locations throughout the story.

Bob and Raydene became lifelong friends with Angel and me. The life lessons that came to me from these two representatives of the Greatest Generation have profoundly impacted my life and my business. My hope is that Bob and Raydene will become your friends as you read. If they do, you will close this book and be impacted with the values of pursuing joy, celebrating relationships, and operating out of common sense.

Be Intentional

In 2003, my wife, Angel, and I moved to a community called The Northshore, just forty minutes north of New Orleans. We didn't know anyone who lived in the area. It's always hard to start over in a new town but especially with zero connections. Louisiana, despite its vast size, felt incredibly small. Everyone knew everyone. When people asked where you went to school, they meant high school. If you weren't from there, they were friendly, but they didn't need new friends.

At the time, I was starting my business, and—knowing that business requires relationships—I began to wonder how I would make it. I knew one truth: People have to eat. I opened my office about a mile from our home. Still, instead of going home for lunch, I intentionally ate at the restaurant next door: The Bistro.

I couldn't afford to eat there every day, but I aimed for lunch meetings at least twice a week. I invited people I met through church or the Rotary Club, desperately trying to understand this new culture. Amid these lunches, I noticed one older gentleman was there almost every time. Sometimes he was alone; sometimes he was with others.

One day, curiosity got the best of me. I asked a server about him. "That's Bob. He's here almost every weekday. Such a sweet man," he said. Another waiter even suggested I introduce myself. "He's a great guy. You're here often enough; you should say hello."

I intentionally waited until a day when Bob was alone.

"Hi, I'm Eric," I said. "I've noticed you eat here almost every day. I've been enjoying the food, but I wondered what you think is best on the menu."

Bob's face lit up with a smile that reached his eyes. "Eric, it's great to meet you. I'm Bob. Bob Prichard. I've seen you here, too, and wondered when you'd come say hello. Why don't you sit down?"

"I didn't mean to interrupt your lunch; I just wanted to meet you."

"No interruption at all," he insisted. "Sit down and join me."

I told him that Angel and I had just moved to town and explained the difficulty we were experiencing in trying to get to know people.

He nodded knowingly. "Forty-five years ago, my wife, Raydene, and I moved here from Oklahoma. It took a few years to make real friendships. Keep trying, but for now, let's eat lunch."

I quickly agreed. Bob recommended the wedge salad with blue cheese, and we both ordered. As the waiter left, Bob added, "And don't forget my cabernet refill."

Bob glanced at me. "Want a glass? The house wine is fantastic."

I thought for a moment. "I'd better not. I have to go back to the office this afternoon."

Bob chuckled. "Eric, so do I, but I've never let that stop me! Are you sure you don't want a glass?"

I laughed and confirmed my decision. Bob's humor was infectious.

As we ate, I asked, "I noticed you're alone today. Does that happen often?"

Bob smiled warmly. "I head out for lunch every day at 11:45. Anyone who wants to join me is always welcome. My daughter, Darcy, works with me, and she often joins. Raydene comes along when she can. Today, I was alone until you showed up, so let's get to know each other."

I told Bob about how Angel and I met at Texas A&M, about our moves around the country, and about the opportunity that landed us in Louisiana. My son Clayton was just over two years old, and Angel was pregnant with our next son, Austen.

Then I asked Bob to tell me about himself. He leaned back thoughtfully. "I grew up in the Oklahoma oil fields. I've been working in the petroleum business in some fashion since I was sixteen. Today, I'm just an old oilman. My wife and I moved here in 1958 when Argo Oil Corporation brought me to town as a division supervisor over Louisiana, Mississippi, Alabama, Arkansas, and Florida. I've been working for myself since 1962. I never expected to stay, but it's hard to leave once the bayou gets in your blood. I still have a few producing oil wells, but we'll shut things down in a few years."

He told me about his family—two daughters, a son who passed away, seven granddaughters, and one grandson. "Family is the most important thing to me," he said.

The waiter brought our salads and Bob's wine. We ate quietly, the silence comfortable. After a few bites, Bob spoke up. "So, tell me about your business."

I paused, not wanting to come across as if I was pitching something. "I recently took over a financial planning and investment business from a family friend who's retiring. It's an opportunity for me to start fresh and do things differently."

Bob raised an eyebrow. "What do you mean by 'do things differently'?"

I thought for a moment. "The big firms tend to be rigid and impersonal. They seem to be consumed with financial outcomes without any regard to the long-term impact those outcomes may have on family relationships. I believe there's a better way—one in which I can help families be more intentional with their wealth and build abundance while making a greater impact."

Bob smiled, taking a sip of his wine. "Eric, I like you. You think like I do. So many of my friends and colleagues have spent their time chasing money while, at the end of the day, ruining their marriage, their relationships with their children, and, in some unfortunate cases, themselves. I don't think the word *intention* gets used enough.

"That's why I take time to eat lunch each day." Bob continued, "It allows me to relax and think or enjoy the company of people I love. And you know what? I truly believe my life has turned out better because I slowed down. Sure, I might have been able to make more money if I hadn't stopped for lunch each day, but at what cost? I haven't met many men with a sense of purpose like you just expressed. We must keep having lunch together."

I was overwhelmed. I felt as if someone other than Angel understood my dream for the first time. "Thank you, Bob. I'd like that a lot."

Bob grinned. "You know I'm here every day. Join me when you can. I'll introduce you to Raydene and Darcy the next time they join me. They'll like you, too."

"I look forward to that. Can I at least buy lunch?" I asked.

"No, I've got a tab here. Lunch is always on me," Bob replied.

I sat in silence, processing everything. Bob picked up his hat. "I've got to get back to the office. I enjoyed today and look forward to doing it again."

He stood up and left. I sat there, wondering who this man was. Little did I know that Bob would become my teacher, mentor, and friend over the next few years.

THE PRICHARD PRINCIPLE: CELEBRATE RELATIONSHIPS—*RETURN ON INTENTION* TRUMPS RETURN ON INVESTMENT

The conversation I had with Bob that day unlocked something profound for me—something I hadn't realized before. Everything I'd been taught in the financial services industry had revolved around achieving financial outcomes. Success was measured in dollars and percentages. But there was no room for relationships in that equation. And that never sat well with me.

Bob helped me see that relationships are the results that truly matter. He introduced me to a different kind of ROI—*return on intention*. It's about aligning your resources and actions with the vision God has placed on your heart rather than chasing numbers that ultimately leave you empty. It's about being intentional with the gifts God has given us—our time, money, and relationships—to create a legacy that reflects His purpose for our lives.

Over the years, I've embraced this principle not only in my work but in my personal life as well. I've learned that when I focus on building meaningful connections and making intentional decisions guided by purpose, amazing things happen. And guess what? Financial outcomes take care of themselves, often exceeding expectations.

Today, I help others shift their focus to *return on intention*, and I see it transform lives. Families communicate better, relationships grow stronger, and the vision for their future becomes clearer. It's not about sacrificing financial growth. It's about approaching it with the right priorities. Bob taught me that abundance is secondary. It's the result of investing in what truly matters: the people we love, the purpose we serve, and the legacy we create.

Family Is Your Top Asset

I did my best to stop by and say hello to Bob often, and we managed to eat together about twice a month. Each lunch was a treasure trove of wisdom as Bob revealed more about his life, family, and purpose.

Bob was born in Oklahoma in 1923, just before the Great Depression. He shared about watching his family lose everything during that time. His father worked in the oil fields and didn't think much about the future. When the Depression hit, they were unprepared. Despite his love for his dad, Bob was deeply hurt by what he perceived as a lack of foresight and care during their time of need. This pain fueled Bob's decision to prioritize his family with a lifelong commitment to planning and intentionality.

Bob's faith became a cornerstone during those challenging times. When he was thirteen, a tent revival came to town, and after attending one night, Bob accepted Christ. By the end of the revival, his entire family had also come to faith. Bob often reflected on that moment, saying, "This is when I first felt a true sense of purpose. God revealed my calling to me, showing me insights in oil production that others couldn't see. This gift would not only support my family but also enable me to help others. No matter how dark life became, I always relied on God's promises."

When Pearl Harbor was bombed in 1941, Bob was an eighteen-year-old senior in high school. The war interrupted his college studies at The University of Oklahoma (OU), where he had begun pursuing a degree in petroleum engineering. In December 1942, Bob enlisted in the Navy and began active duty in July 1943. He trained to fly F6F Hellcats in Michigan and visited home between trainings.

Bob's mom was appointed head of the rationing board during this time. Working alongside her was a woman named Elsie Scott. Elsie's daughter, Raydene, was also working to distribute rations to families.

The Scott family was well-to-do, but Elsie encouraged Raydene to take care of the Prichards when she could because of the high position Bob's mother held. While on leave one time, Bob came through the ration line for meat and tires. Raydene used that opportunity to put her phone number in the back of his rationing book, encouraging Bob to contact her if he needed any extra rations. Although not necessarily a traditional introduction to courtship, it worked for them.

Bob was commissioned as a Naval officer and pilot in April 1945. He and Raydene married that same month, just before he was set to be deployed to the Pacific. Thankfully, the war ended before he saw combat, and by December, he was honorably discharged. Bob then returned to OU to finish his degree. Raydene worked as a receptionist at a local oil company, and Bob used his spare time and summers to work in oil field well servicing. He often said, "I was gifted in the oil business, so why waste time flying planes? I had a family to support, and it was time to get to work."

Bob finally graduated in 1950 and began working as an oil roustabout, maintaining equipment for Republic Natural Gas Company. Bob's reputation for excellence saw him quickly promoted to foreman, then drilling engineer, and eventually division drilling supervisor. These promotions required several moves around Oklahoma, Texas, and Louisiana. It was August 1958 when Argo Oil Corporation saw Bob's potential and hired him as the division supervisor in New Orleans. Bob told me, "Many of the moves were hard on the family, but I knew I had to make Raydene and the kids my priority. I did everything I could to be home for dinner every night, and I even made a point to take Raydene out on a date at least twice a month."

One lunch, Bob shared exciting news: "The whole family is getting together at Darcy's house next month. I'll have three generations of the Prichard family together for the first time in at least five years," he proclaimed with a proud smile.

"I'm thrilled to hear that," I said, genuinely pleased for him.

Then Bob surprised me with an unexpected invitation. "I want you to be there," he said.

I was speechless. "I'm honored," I replied quickly. "But why me?"

"You and I have been talking about my family for so long that it's time you met everyone. If you're the guy to help me manage this last quarter of my life, then you need to know my family."

He had shared so much about his family in conversations. Now he wanted me to be part of it. What had started as friendship was becoming so much more. Bob Prichard was inviting me to plan his legacy. A few weeks later, he gave me the date and time for the gathering, insisting I bring Angel and the boys.

We arrived at Darcy's home in the afternoon, greeted by joyful chaos and the delicious smell of a Southern Louisiana crawfish boil. Bob, ever the gracious host, welcomed us warmly. The scene was vibrant with a palpable sense of family unity: Everyone was chatting and laughing.

I shook Bob's hand and noticed his empty glass.

"Looks like you need more wine," I quipped.

He laughed and said, "How'd you guess?"

"While you are refilling my glass, why don't you get some for yourself? You don't have to go back to the office today, do you?"

I smiled back at him and responded, "Not going to the office today."

"Have some crawfish," Bob's daughter Denna said, handing me a large platter overflowing with food. Clayton, my adventurous eater, quickly commandeered my lap and assigned me the task of cracking open crawfish for him. I couldn't help but absorb the joy and love around me as I focused on the task.

Toward the end of the day, Bob pulled me aside. "Eric, I'm so glad you brought your family today. Look around this backyard and tell me what you see."

I took a moment to observe. His grandson sat by the pool with his mom and aunt, animatedly sharing a story. Four of his granddaughters were playing volleyball. Holding our son Austen in her arms, my wife was chatting with Raydene. Everyone was smiling.

"This is my top asset," Bob began. "All of these people mean the world to me. They are depending on me. When

I look around this yard, I see the educations and down payments on homes I've promised to pay for. Remember this moment when you and I begin working on a plan for my money."

Bob's following words were profound. "I told you about my dad and how he let my family down. I won't allow that to happen again. I want to be intentional about why we are doing everything we choose to do. Money needs to have a purpose. You are looking at my purpose and the most important line item on my balance sheet."

He leaned in, his voice steady and full of conviction. "When I prepare for a workover on a well, I don't just dive in. I craft a plan, prioritizing what truly matters. I've seen others in my field chase dollars without aligning their actions with what's important, and they inevitably come up short. I refuse to let that happen.

"You and I are going to build a plan together. It's not just about ensuring Raydene and I are secure or that we can pay for college and home down payments for all these grandchildren. It's about intentionally creating a pathway that reflects the blessings I want to pour into my family. Without a plan grounded in these values, we're just wandering, missing the opportunity to make a lasting impact."

At that moment, the truth hit me. Bob wasn't talking just about financial security; he was talking about building something far more important. For years, I'd been helping families think through wealth building based on abstract "risk tolerance" scores, neglecting the heart of what truly matters. The real priority wasn't the numbers—it was ensuring families could live out their dreams and values through intentional planning.

From that day on, I committed to ensuring every family I served would have a plan that wasn't just a financial blueprint but a reflection of their deepest desires for their loved ones. I realized why Bob had invited me into his world. He wanted me to see his vision up close—to understand that planning was about more than wealth; it was about living out his dreams with the people he loved most.

I glanced over at Angel, holding both of our boys. My purpose was there as well. I saw a reflection of my own dreams and future. One day, I would sit in a backyard full of my grandchildren. Did I know what I wanted for them? Bob opened my eyes to a truth so clear it's easy to overlook: Our future hinges on having a clear vision, but if we truly want to make an impact, we must recognize that our families are our most important asset. What a tragedy it would be to help someone achieve all their financial goals only to see them lose their family in the process. Bob reinforced the value of a solid plan. He helped me realize that my family isn't just a top priority; it's the greatest investment I'll ever make.

THE PRICHARD PRINCIPLE: CELEBRATE RELATIONSHIPS— FAMILY IS YOUR TOP ASSET

Bob taught me something profound that day in Darcy's backyard: Family isn't just important—it's the most valuable asset we have. Yet, it's rarely on anyone's balance sheet. Too often, we focus on financial goals while unintentionally sacrificing the relationships that matter most.

That moment shifted my perspective. When I work with families now, we start with their vision for the next one hundred years. I ask, "What do you want for your loved ones? What values do you hope to pass on? What legacy do you want to leave?" Once that vision is clear, the financial strategies come into focus.

Personally, Bob's lesson reminded me that my purpose is rooted in the people I love. Whether it's spending intentional time with my wife and children or helping others prioritize their families, I've learned that true abundance isn't about wealth—it's about *relationships*. Families are the greatest investment we'll ever make.

Abundance Defeats Scarcity

Lunch with Bob was a cherished time in my month. We'd gather at our familiar corner table, where the air was filled with the rich scents of fried seafood and Cajun spices. The ambiance was warm, not just because of the cozy setting but also because of the wisdom Bob would share. His stories carried invaluable lessons. Each tale was a testament to the principles that truly matter—faith, family, and intentional living.

Bob swirled his wine and tempted me with a story: "Eric," his eyes twinkling with nostalgia and gravity, "did I ever tell you about crash-landing my F6F Hellcat?"

"No, Bob," I replied, leaning in with anticipation. "Tell me."

Bob's story began during a training exercise in Michigan. His Hellcat's landing gear had malfunctioned, and he circled the airstrip, trying to decide what to do. The fear was palpable. He was going to crash; the question was, Would he survive?

"I had to choose between thinking with fear or thinking with faith," he said, his voice steady but reflective.

Bob paused to sip his wine, allowing the weight of his words to settle in. "I realized that if I let fear take over, I would surely die."

Bob's eyes revealed he was back in the cockpit as he told the story.

"I had a fighting chance. I had to focus on what I had rather than what I lacked."

"What did you have?" I asked, curious to see where this was going.

"You see, I had my knowledge of aerodynamics, a clear runway, and the ability to stay calm," Bob said matter-of-factly. "I had to shift my mindset from scarcity—focusing on what I was missing and what was going wrong—to abundance, recognizing what I had. That shift saved my life."

A smile came over his face, and he chuckled as he continued. "No one else seemed to have my confidence. I saw the ambulance and fire trucks rushing to the runway. But I prayed and began what I can only describe as a controlled crash landing."

He took a long sip of wine and pointed to the sky as he continued. "He heard my prayers. I suffered only some scratches and a mild concussion. The Hellcat, however, wasn't as fortunate."

I realized I had been holding my breath as if I had been in the cockpit with him throughout the whole experience. I exhaled deeply and asked, "Bob, where did you learn to think this way?"

Bob leaned back, his expression thoughtful. "Well, if you don't mind me teaching an old Sunday school lesson. . . . Are you familiar with the story of Jesus and the feeding of the five thousand?"

"Yes," I replied.

"The disciples saw only scarcity and feared they couldn't feed the people. But Jesus asked them, 'What do you have?' and the disciples responded, 'We have five loaves and two fish.' Jesus knew what was possible through God and told the disciples to have the people sit down. About five thousand men, possibly as many as fifteen thousand total people, including women and children, had an excellent and filling meal. The disciples then picked up twelve baskets of leftovers."

Bob glanced at me to see if I was with him.

"God's abundance was more than they began with. When your mindset starts with what you have, you always see a greater possibility. Ever since I heard that story of the loaves and fishes, I've tried to be grateful for what I have. That mindset saved my life that day."

For a moment, my mind drifted to my own experiences from the past.

"Bob," I started, "You've reminded me of a similar story Angel and I experienced. When Angel was pregnant with Clayton, we wanted her to stay home instead of working. However, our budget was always $200 short each month. We tried cutting out every extra expense but couldn't get the $200 deficit to disappear.

"We prayed and made the commitment for Angel to stay home, but to be truly in alignment with God, we also committed to giving our 10 percent. We didn't have a church at the time, so much of our giving was to food banks, women's shelters, and other opportunities that God would put in front of us as we asked Him to open our eyes.

"There was an opportunity to be scared. We were $200 short. *Where would we get the money to cover our deficit and the tithe God asked for?* we wondered. But we had our family, our faith, and our instruction from God for

Angel to stay home, so we trusted He would take care of us.

"That year, we paid off $7,000 in debt and never missed out on anything. We still don't know where the extra money came from, but living with an abundance mindset left us wealthier than living in scarcity."

Bob nodded, a knowing look in his eyes. "That's the power of abundance," he said. "When you focus on what you have and trust in God's provision, the results can be miraculous."

As we finished our lunch, I found myself in a reflective mood. My friendship with Bob Prichard was having a profound impact on my life. Each tale was a stepping stone, leading me to see the value of relationships, joy, and common sense. Like seeds planted in fertile soil, Bob's principles took root in my heart.

"Thank you, Bob," I said, grateful for his wisdom.

"Anytime, Eric," he replied with a smile I had come to appreciate. "Remember, always see what you have."

"I see that I have an empty wine glass."

"An opportunity for more wine!" He laughed out loud.

As lunch ended, Bob's words echoed in my mind. His stories were more than just anecdotes. They were life lessons wrapped in the warmth of shared wisdom. Each lunch with Bob peeled back layers of fear and doubt, revealing a core of truth that guided me in my personal and professional life. The principle of seeing what you have and embracing abundance became a beacon for me, leading me to a place of gratitude and peace.

THE PRICHARD PRINCIPLE: PURSUE JOY—ABUNDANCE DEFEATS SCARCITY

Bob's story of surviving a crash landing stuck with me, not just because it was dramatic but because it revealed something profound: the power of focusing on what we *have* instead of what we lack. That simple shift in mindset—choosing abundance over scarcity—can change everything. These days, I've learned to start my day by asking, "What do I have?" rather than getting tripped up by what I lack. Honestly, it's one reason I ignore my newsfeed. The media focuses on fear and lack, which pulls me away from the gratitude and clarity I need to thrive.

What Bob shared made me realize how often a scarcity mindset leads to fear. When we're focused on what we don't have, we end up feeling like there's not enough to go around. That fear pushes us to protect ourselves and our families, but in doing so, it reinforces the cycle of scarcity. It's something I've seen countless times in the financial world, where the focus on limited resources often causes people to miss out on the bigger picture.

Bob helped me see that when we begin with abundance—trusting that God provides what we need—we gain a sense of peace. That peace allows us to think clearly, make better decisions, and focus on the impact we want to have on the world.

This shift doesn't just bring peace; it opens up new possibilities. When I think abundantly, I'm not just protecting my family—I'm partnering with God to create lasting impact. That perspective not only gives me hope for today, but it also inspires me to think generationally, building a legacy that reflects His provision and love for the world. Abundance defeats scarcity, but more importantly, it invites us into a bigger story of faith and purpose.

Be an Owner

It was a bright, sunny afternoon as Bob, his youngest daughter, Darcy, and I settled into our usual corner booth at The Bistro. The waiter, familiar with our routine, brought over Bob's favorite bottle of wine. The clinking of glasses and the hum of conversation created a comfortable backdrop as we settled in, anticipating good food and a hearty serving of wisdom.

Bob leaned back in his chair, a nostalgic smile on his lips. "Eric, I wasn't always a business owner," he began. "As you may remember, we moved to New Orleans forty-five years ago, when Darcy was one, to work for Argo Oil Corporation. It was a stable job, something you could count on. But stability isn't always enough."

Darcy nodded thoughtfully, her interest clearly piqued. "I remember bits and pieces of your early days in the oil fields, but I don't think I've ever heard the whole story of how you came to own a business," she said.

Bob chuckled. "That's because it's a story filled with fear, risk, and a lot of faith." He took a sip of his wine. "I met a man at Argo named Mullins—I always called him Mullins, but for the longest time I didn't know if it was his first or last name. He was brilliant and could see opportunities where others saw obstacles.

"Mullins had a keen eye for getting broken and non-working wells back online—wells that could be bought for next to nothing.

"And I had a knack for finding opportunities others had given up on.

"One day, in 1962, Mullins came to me with a crazy idea: 'Bob,' he said, 'did you hear that Argo has been sold? We keep working for these companies that keep changing hands; why should we keep making them money? With your ability to find the wells and my engineering expertise, it's a match made in oil field heaven. We can own a business and take care of our families.'

"I was scared," Bob admitted. "Leaving the perceived stability of the corporate world, especially with three young children, was terrifying.

"The oil market wasn't forgiving, and there wasn't much margin for error."

At this point, Darcy chimed in, her voice filled with emotion. "I was pretty young, Dad—no older than five—but I remember feeling safe."

She grabbed her father's hand and looked into his eyes with appreciation.

"You were brave, and that bravery made us feel secure."

Tears formed in her eyes as she continued, "I didn't realize then how much faith you had in yourself."

"It wasn't faith in myself that kept me going," Bob interrupted. "It was your mom. She was my rock.

"Raydene believed in me even when I didn't believe in myself. She kept saying, 'Bet on yourself, Bob. Trust in God.'

"Your mother opened my eyes to the parable of the ten minas in the Bible. I still have the Bible in which she underlined portions to get my attention. She ensured I noticed when Jesus said, 'Do business until I return.'

"I can still hear her words: 'Bob, even Jesus thinks you need to own a business!'

"For months, I felt like I was back in junior high Sunday school as she showed me how the first servant made ten times the amount he was given, and the second made five.

"'Bob, you and Mullins are gifted!' she proclaimed. 'I trust you to take care of us.'"

Bob grew quiet as he reflected on Raydene's lessons. In a whispered voice, he told us the next part of the story. "But the real catalyst for my final decision happened when Raydene said, 'Bob if you don't do this, you risk burying your gift like the third servant. Use it, and it will multiply.'"

Bob paused to take a sip of cabernet before he continued.

"So, we took the plunge. Mullins and I bought our first few wells for pennies on the dollar. It was a risk, a leap of faith into the unknown.

"The oil market was tough, and the prices kept declining for several years. But Raydene's unwavering faith kept us going."

Before Darcy or I could interrupt, Bob's face changed from reflective to exuberant.

"For over ten years, we kept plugging along, making just enough money to stay open and pay our bills.

"Then, in late 1973, the OPEC oil embargo hit. Oil prices skyrocketed almost fourfold just as we bought our twentieth well into the portfolio. Being an owner paid off," Bob said, a glimmer of triumph in his eyes. "Instead of just collecting paychecks, we intentionally created wealth for our families. It was hard, but our abundance mindset had rewarded us again."

I leaned in, feeling the weight of Bob's story. "Bob, your story resonates with me. When Angel encouraged me to own this financial practice, I was terrified. We had saved six months' worth of expenses to cover our family's needs while the business was getting off the ground.

"During my prayer times," I continued, "God kept challenging me with one question: 'Do you trust Me?'

"I kept exploring what this meant, and as I prayed through it, I felt God challenging me with another question: 'Do *you* own this business, or do *I* own this business?'

"This led to a series of challenging conversations with God.

"'Why do you ask?' I questioned Him. 'If You own this business, then do what You want.'

"God shared, 'If I own this business, then I need you to do something for Me.'

"'You own this business,' I replied, somewhat hesitantly, because I didn't know what was coming.

"'Then I'll tell you that you saved too much money for this business to be successful,' God shared with me. 'If you go forward with this much in the bank, you will be tempted to think that the blessings waiting for you came because of you rather than Me.'

"'How much is too much?' I questioned.

"'I need you to give away half of what you've saved!' God shared.

"This experience was hard on several fronts. *Was I hearing from God, or was my mind playing tricks on me? I* thought. *And what would Angel think?*

"When I shared this with Angel, she agreed to pray. But it wasn't long until she shared that this was God's plan for us.

"Clayton and Austen were still young, and I would be lying if I didn't say I carried doubts about how I would provide for my family. But, just as Raydene believed in you, Angel believed in me, and it gave me hope for moving forward.

"Together, we prayed over where to give this money, and I can still remember how hard my hand was shaking as I wrote a check to an orphanage in Russia.

"But, like you said, Bob, I can see that God has provided everything we've needed. Having an owner's mindset has changed my perspective."

Bob smiled, his eyes twinkling with understanding. "Eric, people often say we're just lucky. But luck favors the bold.

"I suppose those who trust in God and take risks seem to find luck in life. But we're not lucky; we're blessed because we're bold enough to trust Him."

Darcy had been listening intently, but she had been quiet throughout her father's story and mine.

Finally, she spoke up. "Dad, I don't feel I'm meant to own a business. How can I use these concepts for my own family?"

Bob smiled warmly. "Darcy, you don't have to run a business to own one.

"The stock market is a fancy name given to a marketplace of businesses that are already thriving. There are thousands of successful existing businesses you can own a piece of—and the best part is, you don't have to be involved in the day-to-day operations.

"Not everyone will be called to run a business outright, like Eric and me. But everyone has the opportunity to get a piece of the ownership pie. And that's how generational abundance is created."

Darcy thoughtfully replied, "That's great, but it sounds overwhelming. How would I even know where to start?"

Bob gently grabbed my arm for emphasis and continued, "That's what Eric does. He helps you sift through the thousands of businesses to own the right mix that can intentionally bless your family.

"He's helping your mother and me as we're selling these wells out of my business and moving our dollars into other successful existing businesses.

"The principle of ownership is the same, but I'm now in a season in which I want to shift from running the business. Eric is helping me ensure I can spend more time with the family, enjoying life and more lunches with good wine."

As our lunch ended, Bob invited Darcy to join us more often. "Eric and I are creating a plan, not just for what we own but for how we can be more intentional as a family. I know our conversations will help you learn how to continue blessing my grandchildren."

I had a deep sense of gratitude for Bob's mentorship. As I walked away from lunch, I felt a renewed excitement for the future. God had placed me in a unique position. I was able to own a business, and that business was also in the position of helping others discover how their journey of ownership could create abundance for their family. My work could have an intentional impact for generations, and I always left our lunches remembering that truth.

THE PRICHARD PRINCIPLE:
USE COMMON SENSE—THINK LIKE AN OWNER

Bob's story reminded me of a truth I've come to value deeply: Much of the world's wealth has been created because someone chose to take the leap into business ownership. At its core, owning a business isn't solely about profits—it's about serving and loving others. The most successful businesses thrive by providing products or services that enhance lives. Ownership gives us the chance to play an active role in that impact. The more we focus on serving others, the more the business can grow—and the more opportunities we create for our families and communities.

That said, not everyone is called to run a business, and that's OK. Bob taught me that ownership can take many forms. The stock market, for instance, is simply a marketplace of businesses in which anyone can own a piece of a company that's already thriving. It's less about taking on daily operations and more about thinking like an owner—choosing to invest in businesses that prioritize serving others. The headlines may make investing seem risky, but when we focus on businesses with a long-term vision of impact and service, the results often reflect that same intentionality.

In my work today, I help families shift their perspective to embrace this owner's mindset. Instead of being distracted by the constant noise of market fluctuations, we focus on identifying businesses that are creating lasting value for their customers and their communities. It's this focus on intentional ownership that not only creates financial growth but also lays the foundation for generational wealth.

Bob and Raydene right after they were married

*Bob in his Air
Force pilot gear*

*Bob in his F6F
Hellcat*

Bob loved the outdoors

Raydene, Darcy, Scott, Bob, and Dena

Bob, Darcy, and Raydene

Bob, Raydene, and their "top asset"

Bob fishing on a rare cold day in Louisiana

Bob and Raydene at a dinner event I hosted

Bob (This is the man I remember!)

Me (Eric) sitting behind Bob's desk

Distraction Leads to Erosion

It had been almost two years since we met, and Bob and I had settled into our lunch routine, meeting twice a month. One warm Monday, as spring was turning into summer, I arrived to find my friend swirling his wine, his eyes revealing that he was far off in a blissful memory.

As I sat down, Bob invited me into his thoughts.

"Raydene and I were down at Grand Isle this weekend, Eric. I love having a sanctuary to get away and intentionally reflect. I saw two dolphins out in the Gulf and caught several redfish. We also trapped some crabs off the boat dock.

"I ate like a king!" he exclaimed.

Bob and Raydene loved spending weekends at their fishing camp, a modest vacation home two hours south of New Orleans on Route 1. From their front porch, they could watch waves roll in and spot center console fishing boats navigating the waters of the Gulf of Mexico. Monday lunches inevitably included fishing stories from his Grand Isle neighbors and descriptions of the colorful rainbows that often followed the afternoon rainstorms.

"Do you know what I love most about my time at the camp?" Bob asked rhetorically before sharing his thoughts.

"I love how it allows me to slow down and focus on what's important. I sit and think. I have deep conversations with Raydene. I take time to appreciate the sunsets. "When I'm working, I'm caught up in the distractions. I don't see the flowers that are blooming or the changing of the seasons.

"And in life, these distractions often have the highest cost."

I pondered how I had experienced this myself and processed how to respond when Bob continued.

"As I was driving Raydene home on Sunday evening, I made the mistake of turning on a talk radio show. They commented that the economy isn't doing well and the stock market is down.

"In less than thirty minutes after leaving my sanctuary, I was distracted, and my focus had shifted. I had let someone else move my mindset from abundance to scarcity.

"Have I told you about my adventures as a used car salesman?" Bob asked.

The question caught me off guard. I had no idea where he was going next.

"No, Bob," I responded. "But I'm curious."

"In 1948, Raydene and I lived in student housing at OU. We needed extra money, so between classes, I washed cars and did minor maintenance at an auto dealership. It was just after World War II, and the economy was experiencing slow growth and high inflation.

"Raydene did her best to keep us focused on gratitude and abundance, but the newspaper, radio, and peers at the struggling auto dealer kept tempting me with the distraction of current events.

"One morning, I was reading the local newspaper and came across an article about car prices in California. Inflation and inventory shortages were causing prices to be almost double what I saw on the local lot.

"I had a trailer I could rent and knew I could buy two or three cars in Oklahoma, drive them to California, and make a good profit. While everyone else was distracted, I found an opportunity."

"How did it go?" I asked.

"Extremely well," Bob replied. "I made two trips, with three cars each time. I doubled my money on the first trip and did a little better than that on my second.

"You remember when we talked about the importance of ownership, and I mentioned how Raydene loved the parable of the talents so much that she marked up my Bible?"

I nodded and smiled.

"I've always thought about that third servant who buried his talent. He was distracted by fear. Any of my peers in Oklahoma could have done what I did, but they were focused on the wrong things. Their fear was expensive."

"I feel like we see this almost every hurricane season," I spoke up, reflecting on the period from July to September when most of us watch the weather report like a gambling junkie watches a high-stakes game of poker.

"How much news is consumed speculating that the next big storm could cause more erosion along the Louisiana coast? When there is a real threat, we respond. But how many days have been lost by families and businesses distracted by a storm that may go somewhere else?"

Bob shook his head and replied, "If I were focused on hurricanes and erosion, we wouldn't have our camp in Grand Isle. We have a generator, and we leave town when the threat is real, but it's foolish to be focused on what could go wrong to the point that we miss the joy of the camp."

"Bob, can I ask you a question?"

"Go ahead," he said, tilting his wine glass in my direction.

"You mentioned how tough the economy was for you and Raydene at OU. It sounds a little like what we've been experiencing the last few years. Would you agree?" I asked, genuinely interested in his thoughts.

"I think I see some similarities in the economy, but mostly I see similarities in the distractions." Then he paused to let his words sit before continuing.

"Today, it's not just the newspapers; you have a twenty-four-hour news cycle that constantly invites you to focus on the wrong things.

"We were talking about erosion earlier. Do you know what erosion no one talks about?"

"What, Bob?" I responded, leaning in to see where this was going.

"The erosion of inflation," Bob started.

"Our lunch today cost more than Raydene and I would spend on a week of groceries at OU. Just as the storms erode the coastline, inflation erodes our financial stability. It's a gradual process, almost invisible at first. But, over time, it's expensive and can cause significant damage.

"All the news these last few years has been focused on the stock market's ups and downs and how the economy is doing. We live in one of the greatest countries in the world. There may be temporary bad news, but we've always been resilient and found a way to thrive. Why would this time be any different?

"The greatest truth I've observed is that being an owner keeps you ahead of inflation. Owning those cars and my business has kept me ahead of any economic erosion during my lifetime. I expect we will continue to see the same thing as we own the right companies and continue to build the plan for my family."

"I've noticed this as well, Bob," I interjected. "The financial news media seems to thrive off of keeping investors distracted, and it's easy to see how most people are losing generational wealth because of the fear that seems so prevalent in the messages. I'm wondering how much money the average person misses out on because they are distracted."

With a wink and a grin, Bob said, "If they were focused, they probably would have a fishing camp where they could drink wine and enjoy life."

Our lunch ended soon after, but the conversation lingered in my mind. Bob's wisdom wasn't just about money; it was a deeper understanding of life. Slowing down to concentrate on family and abundance was the key to staying focused. I knew that the erosion of wealth was a real threat we had to navigate on behalf of families like Bob's, but I also planned to spend more time preparing to keep my head clear of distractions. We didn't have a fishing camp yet, but I knew Angel and I needed to find our sanctuary.

THE PRICHARD PRINCIPLE:
USE COMMON SENSE–AVOID EROSION

Living on the Gulf Coast, erosion is a daily reality. Like many of our neighbors, Angel and I donate our Christmas trees each year to help rebuild the marshes and coastlines. But Bob helped me see erosion in a different light. He connected it to inflation—a gradual loss of financial stability that, like coastal erosion, happens so slowly you almost don't notice it until the damage is done. His insight shifted my perspective on what truly threatens a family's financial legacy.

In the investment world, so much focus is placed on managing market risk, but Bob's wisdom pointed me toward the real risk: the erosion of purchasing power. The cost of everyday essentials—bread, milk, gas—rises every year, and the past few years (2021–2024) have brought inflation levels we haven't seen in decades. As I studied different strategies, I found that the best way to stay ahead of inflation was through ownership—investing in individual companies. Bonds and gold couldn't keep up, but owning businesses through the stock market offered a path to protect and grow purchasing power.

This isn't always easy, though. Inflation creeps in slowly, while the ups and downs of the stock market can feel like a roller coaster. That's where I see distraction becoming the real enemy. Families lose generational wealth not because of bad investments but because they're distracted by short-term fears and immediate gratification. Bob's perspective helped me focus on the long term—on how owning the right companies can help families not only preserve but grow their wealth over time.

Diversification Is *Di-worse-ification*

Eventually Bob became more than just a friend; he was my mentor. He made me think and challenged me to be a better version of myself. His keen eyes always seemed to penetrate straight into my thoughts.

"How's business going?" he asked one day when I had barely slid into my seat.

I pushed my unneeded menu aside and took a moment to reflect before answering.

"Bob, I feel like you and I have been friends forever—but it's only been a couple of years, right?" My friend blinked and nodded. His eyes perceived I was about to share something personal.

"Every day that I leave one of our lunches, I spend time intentionally reflecting on our conversation, sometimes for several days."

Pausing to gather my thoughts allowed Bob time to take a sip of wine. I continued, "We both know that being an owner is the best path to wealth and avoiding the erosion caused by inflation. But here's the thing: Not everyone agrees with you and me.

"I receive countless calls and emails from prominent research groups and big names on Wall Street, all tossing around technical terms like *diversification, volatility,* and *alpha,* as if the complexity of their language proves their ability to serve my client families. Yet, the deeper I dive into their research, the more it feels like a sales pitch disguised as education; it lacks the true substance and clarity my families deserve.

"The products they offer encourage a mindset of fear and scarcity. No one seems to provide solutions focused on generational abundance. Something is off."

Bob took it in—pausing in an unhurried way and then nodded. "I'm just an old oilman, Eric, but my old friend common sense whispers a different kind of research. He says, 'Look for the solutions you need, and know when it's time to create your own.'"

Bob leaned back, and that familiar spark ignited in his eyes. I knew I was in for one of Bob's stories from the past. He began recounting how, in the early days, brokers would frequently approach him and Mullins, eager to sell oil wells out of their inventory. "Oh, they had a lot of wells and even more stories about why their wells were better than any others available. However, we learned that doing our own research helped us understand industry trends that were far more valuable. We had built strong relationships, and firsthand research led us to find opportunities before they ever hit the market."

He paused, taking a sip of his wine. "Doing our own research cut out these brokers, and we made more money. Over the long term, we could build a profitable business because we understood the marketplace."

Immediately I knew what I needed to do: "If I can't find what I need, I need to do my own research."

It was half a question and half a statement.

Bob, grinning so big I could see his crooked teeth all the way back to his molars, said, "Exactly. I can't wait to see what you and my friend common sense discover."

For the next two weeks, I borrowed books from the local library, downloaded audiobooks and videos, and spent hours with my nose in the computer as I pored over research. Angel held down the fort, knowing I was onto something significant. She also gently urged me to take breaks to be there for our children, Clayton and Austen. Our third baby was on the way, and I knew Angel and I wanted to prioritize our growing family. After giving my kids their evening baths and reading bedtime stories, I slipped away to my home office, where Angel often fell asleep in my recliner as I worked late into the night.

While I knew that this research project was important, I also had promised Angel and the boys that I would build a sandbox before the new baby arrived. The architect juices were flowing, and the whole family collaborated on the final design. I could have outsourced the building of it, but I learned a valuable lesson while taking on both projects at the same time: Discovering how to serve someone for their best outcomes is a deep expression of joy.

Bob was guiding me to see that what I was searching for was one of the greatest gifts I could give to my family and clients.

Two weeks after our initial "common sense" conversation, I strode into The Bistro with a pile of papers, several dog-eared books, and a broad smile. My steps were purposeful, the gait of someone who has conquered challenges and stands ready for more. Bob and Darcy were already seated.

"I've found so many unique things. Where to start?" I began before I could drop my research collection and take a seat.

I had caught Bob with a mouthful of his Cobb salad and hadn't realized it. He finished his bite and took a quick drink of water to clear his throat. Bob introduced Darcy to the research project I had been working on. Then he looked at me and said, "Let's start with what surprised you the most."

"I'm surprised you're drinking water," I stated, as I realized he didn't have a wine glass in front of him.

Darcy waved her hand at me, saying, "It's no big deal. Daddy has some doctor appointments this week, and they asked him to avoid alcohol for a couple of days.

"And before he gets you too distracted with all this business talk, how is Angel feeling? I can't wait to meet that sweet baby. I'll be sure to make myself available to babysit when you guys want to go out."

"That would be great. Clayton and Austen really enjoy it when you come over," I responded.

"As for Angel, she's tired, but we're all excited to watch our family grow."

Bob waved us both off and said, "You know how much I love this relationship talk, but I want to hear what you discovered. I'm already depressed over my lack of wine, and this sounds like the distraction I need."

We all laughed at his comment, and I began, "Remember how suspicious I was with all the technical terms those big-name groups kept using?"

Bob nodded, and Darcy leaned in with curiosity.

"One point they kept emphasizing was the hundreds of businesses they owned in their products and how important that was for diversification.

"In one of my late-night expeditions, I found a paper by two prominent economists that showed that forty to seventy businesses were enough to keep a family diversified.[1]

"There's a lot of disparity between hundreds and seventy," I finished.

"I'm not surprised," Bob said with a grin.

"This sounds like what Mullins and I discovered. Seventy sounds manageable. When you own hundreds of businesses, you need a lot more help. That help would come at a cost those Wall Street groups would be happy to provide, which sounds expensive."

I interrupted before Bob could say anything else: "It's funny you should mention the expense.

"As I looked into these products, I was shocked at how expensive they were."

"How expensive are they?" Darcy asked, leaning in further.

"There are a lot of complexities in that answer. But I like to keep things simple," I began, focusing specifically on Darcy.

"By my estimates, every million you invest would have an extra expense of $50,000 over a ten-year period when you use the Wall Street products."

Bob choked on his water as I shared this.

"$50,000 is how much Ms. Raydene needs for that new black GMC Yukon Denali with leather interior and chrome wheels she's been eyeing," Bob responded, once he regained his voice.

Then Bob laughed and hit his hand on the table, saying, "This doesn't sound like diversification at all.

"It sounds like *di-worse-ification*."

We all started laughing at his comment, and as things settled down, I repeated it to him, "*Di-worse-ification*. I like the sound of that!

"This process helped me see that the goal of my efforts is to discover how to better serve the people I love and care about.

"It's interesting to think about how many of my colleagues haven't done any research on this. They're taking money from their friends and families, and they're putting it into the hands of the people they work for, and I doubt they realize what it's costing the people they love."

Bob smiled with kind eyes. "Eric, this is why I like you. You're genuinely concerned about my family and my results. I'm proud of you for working hard and uncovering uncomfortable realities. And yes, at the end of the day, the research is about service."

He paused, his eyes reflecting a deeper thought. "You know, I love to play Sunday school teacher when possible. The book of Hosea says, 'My people are destroyed for lack of knowledge.'[2]

"How many of your colleagues spend time seeking knowledge? Your work is going to bless my family for generations. But many of your peers and other families may suffer from less-than-ideal results because they choose not to seek the wisdom intentionally."

I glanced at my watch and realized we had been at lunch for over an hour and a half. "Bob, I didn't know how long we had been here. I'm about to be late for a meeting back at my office."

Bob held up his empty glass and said, "All the more reason for us to have lunch again. And this time, we shouldn't wait two weeks."

I had a profound realization as I hurriedly gathered my papers and books, hoping my next meeting would forgive my tardiness. Bob wasn't just a client; he was an incredible friend. His family and mine were intimately connected. He always imparted invaluable wisdom, and his commonsense approach to life changed and challenged me in all the right ways.

THE PRICHARD PRINCIPLE:
USE COMMON SENSE–AVOID
DI-WORSE-IFICATION

One of the biggest surprises in my career has been discovering how simplicity often outperforms complexity. In the financial world, we hear constant talk about diversification, often framed with fancy terms and layers of complication. But as Bob helped me see, complexity isn't always designed to serve families. It's often designed to benefit the financial industry. This realization challenged me to step back and apply a little common sense.

Owning part of forty to seventy companies could yield better results than owning hundreds. This seemed too good to be true at first. After all, diversification was drilled into me during my training and exams. But when I put it to the test, I was amazed. Not only did the portfolio perform well, but I also saw how much we could save families by cutting out the extra layers of cost baked into more complex financial products. The simplicity of owning fewer businesses gave families clarity and confidence while delivering solid results.

What's more, I've found that families genuinely enjoy knowing more about the companies they own. With fewer than seventy businesses in their portfolio, it becomes manageable and personal. This approach shifts the conversation from overwhelming jargon to something meaningful—helping families understand how their investments align with their goals and vision.

Research Reveals Opportunity

A few days later, I received a call from Darcy, and her voice was filled with anticipation: "Daddy wants to know when you are coming to lunch again," she said.

"How about today?" I asked.

"You know we'll be there," Darcy replied. "See you then—and tell Angel and the boys I say hello."

I was running late as I walked into The Bistro, still carrying the books and papers from all my research. Bob was halfway through a glass of wine and had a half-eaten salad sitting in front of him.

"Already started?" I said with a mischievous grin.

"When Darcy mentioned you'd be here today, I couldn't help but leave the office early. I've been eager to continue our conversation." He flashed his crooked smile, his excitement palpable.

Darcy shrugged and said, "I told you he was excited."

I slid my research to the side of the table and sat down, interested in what Bob was so worked up about.

"So, tell me what you've been thinking," I prompted.

It was good to see Bob drinking wine again as he said, "I realized I told you why Mullins and I did what we did, but I never explained how we did it."

I failed to notice the omission previously. Now I was all ears.

Bob started, "Mullins and I began our business together because I could see the opportunities, and he had the engineering skills to maximize each opportunity.

"We spent hours carefully analyzing data from various wells. Topographical maps gave us insights into the type of drilling required for each project, as soil structure dictates optimal drilling practices. We also leveraged marketplace trends to estimate workover costs, ensuring we maximized profitability in each opportunity.

"Our dedication to research made us more successful investors. Mullins and I frequently discovered projects abandoned due to incomplete or inaccurate assumptions. Our greatest opportunities often came when the revelation of our research trumped expert opinion."

He paused and drained his wine glass. "Does what I'm saying make sense?"

I leaned in and said, "It definitely does, Bob. This is one of the reasons I was excited for us to get back together. If we are focused on owning no more than seventy companies, then most of my efforts should be focused on research."

Bob smiled and nodded knowingly. As the waiter refilled his wine glass, Bob glanced curiously at me and asked, "Where did you start?"

"Well, Bob, you and I have been having lunch together long enough; I thought that would be obvious," I answered with a smile. "I started with common sense!"

Darcy leaned forward and interrupted before I could continue.

"That's not an answer," she stated with mild frustration. "I feel like you two are making inside jokes while I'm trying to learn."

"I'm sorry," I started, still chuckling to myself a little and winking at Bob. "I promise to get to the point.

"Stated simply, it comes down to owning the right businesses at the right time.

"Two books caught my attention about owning the right companies. *Good to Great*, by Jim Collins, and *The Infinite Game*, by Simon Sinek. Both books explore the concept that every business is built with either a short-term or a long-term focus. The businesses with the greatest opportunity to thrive prioritize long-term outcomes, but a short-term focus may create temporary wins that endear you to Wall Street. It's not always obvious which focus company leadership is prioritizing. Still, with intentional research, you can discover if a company is more short-term or long-term focused, and the investment conclusions become more discernable."

I looked at Darcy and asked, "Does this make sense so far?"

"I think so, but if you had a real-world example, that might help," she replied.

"Sure," I started. "You know how the boys are looking forward to their new baby sister coming in the next six months?"

"Yes," Darcy responded, "I can't wait to spoil her."

"Well, Angel and I need a new car to hold everyone," I continued. "When we started shopping, there were a lot of vehicles that could have solved our need short-term. But we settled on a Toyota Sequoia, which was $10,000 over my initial budget, because the safety and longevity ratings were more important for the long-term needs of our family."

"That makes a lot of sense," Darcy responded. "You can't make a decision on a business or anything else if you look only at the short-term outcomes."

I paused and looked at Bob with my mouth open. She had surprised me, but Darcy was beginning to understand.

"Exactly. And we don't just need to own the right companies; we need to own them at the right time," I continued.

"The economic environment will reveal opportunities and pitfalls. For example, while interest rates are low, it's OK for a business to make profits using extra debt. However, if interest rates rise, a business that uses a lot of leverage could find its profits eaten up by debt repayment.

"This isn't everything I found in my research, but if we keep the process simple and focused on common sense, your family can enjoy the blessing of business ownership without the distractions that Wall Street keeps trying to create."

Bob smiled, "Eric, I really like this. You have a lot of Mullins and me in you."

Darcy nodded in agreement and said, "This is so interesting. Thank you for helping me understand something that has always seemed difficult."

"I've got one more thing I would like to show you, if you have a little extra time," I said, holding up a finger.

Bob nodded for me to go ahead.

"In everything I was researching, I kept thinking about the erosion of inflation," I started.

"We agree that owning the right companies at the right time would be part of the fight against this erosion.

In addition, I discovered that quality businesses, which pay dividends, typically increase their yearly payment by more than inflation."

Bob sat back and said slowly, "I don't think I knew that, but tell me more about what you mean."

I continued, "Well, when you need income, most people will buy a bond or a certificate of deposit, right?"

"Sure, I probably wouldn't do that, but I've seen others make that decision," Bob acknowledged.

"I want to keep this as simple as possible," I started, "so let's look at what you could earn from a bond. Probably no more than 6 percent, which means on a $500,000 investment, you could earn $30,000 a year for you and Raydene. Do you agree with those numbers?"

Bob nodded, so I continued.

"The challenge is that with inflation, in ten short years, $30,000 is the same as $21,900 today, and you get only your original $500,000 back at the end."[3]

"And that's why I don't like bonds," Bob said emphatically while looking at Darcy.

"I really think you both will like this," I began.

"Good businesses grow their dividend payout by 5.8 percent each year.[4]

"The average dividend is around 3 percent, so you would need a $1 million investment to earn the same $30,000 the first year. However, by year ten, you would receive $53,500 in income each year, and the value will most likely have grown to $1.8 million.

"The right businesses, at the right time, with the right structure, will reveal the right opportunity to bless your family."

I sat back slowly and enjoyed the moment as it all sunk in.

Bob looked up thoughtfully and grinned. "Eric, this is the type of research Mullins and I would have had a lot of fun with. You're a great student and teacher."

He then looked at Darcy and said, "Do you see how important this is for our family and our future abundance? Most people have forgotten to use common sense in decision-making."

Darcy responded softly, "I see it. This is the mindset we need to protect the legacy you and Momma started."

I was emotionally spent from all the anticipation of sharing my research and conclusions with Bob and Darcy. I started to tear up and could only respond, "Thank you."

We wrapped up lunch shortly after that, and I took the rest of the day off. I went home and spent time with Angel and the boys. I was learning the importance of taking time to think. Still, more importantly, I was learning that relationships matter above all. I knew my opportunities to spend time with my children would go by faster than I could imagine.

THE PRICHARD PRINCIPLE: USE COMMON SENSE—USE RESEARCH TO REVEAL OPPORTUNITIES

At our lunches, Bob picked up on my natural curiosity—and he harnessed that curiosity by pushing me to research to reveal opportunities.

I've always been curious by nature, never one to accept something at face value without digging deeper. Early in my career, this made things challenging when someone brought me a product or idea to share with clients. I had too many questions—often more than they were ready to answer. But when I began doing my own research, it became a source of joy. It felt like solving a puzzle, piecing together trends and using common sense to find opportunities others might overlook.

What struck me the most was how obvious some of these trends seemed when you stepped back and avoided overcomplicating things. For instance, during the pandemic, it was clear that leisure industries like hotels, airlines, and restaurants would struggle, while businesses focused on home life and online shopping would thrive. By focusing on those shifts, we made intentional choices that served families well during a challenging time. The insights weren't hidden—they just required the willingness to see the world through a lens of curiosity and simplicity.

Today, one of my favorite lessons to share is the power of dividends. They're like rent payments for owning a piece of a company. Just as real estate owners collect rental income, dividends provide consistent returns while weathering short-term market ups and downs. Helping families understand this concept has been a game changer. It keeps them focused on long-term opportunities rather than being distracted by the noise of financial media.

When Bob pushed me to research, I learned that the answers are often right in front of us if we're willing to look. God equips us with the tools to see the opportunities all around us, and while it may take extra time and effort, the reward is worth it. There's a deep joy in helping families put the pieces together to build generational abundance, and it's a passion that continues to fuel me every day.

Be Courageous When Others Are Fearful

A couple months went by with Bob absent from our usual lunch routine. I called his office, and Darcy attributed his absence to a handful of routine medical checkups.

When we finally met, Bob suddenly stopped eating mid-lunch, smiled, and asked, "What are you and Angel doing this Saturday night?"

"We have young kids, Bob," I replied. "If we've got anything planned, it probably involves a Disney movie and pepperoni pizza."

He chuckled, "Raydene and I want to take you to dinner. And before you say no, remember, we get only so many Saturday nights to go out.

"We've already talked to Darcy, and she's available to babysit."

When I mentioned it to Angel, she was excited. The kids were excited, too. Darcy was their favorite sitter; she spoiled them like an aunt.

That Saturday night, Angel and I met Bob and Raydene at Magnolia Bay, a nice restaurant in town. They had started on a bottle of Cabernet and were seated in a corner.

As we sat down, Bob offered to fill our glasses.

"Shame on you, Bob," Angel teased, "You just want to dull my senses so I don't keep you and Eric from talking business all night. Besides," she said, patting her baby bump, "I'm looking out for our next generation!"

Bob blushed and winked at Angel, "Fair enough! And I have no intention of talking business *all* night."

Raydene turned to Angel, saying, "I'm glad we get more time together. I love the kids, but adult conversations are nice too."

Angel nodded, and Raydene continued, "Bob says I'm missing some great lunch conversations, but my women's group keeps me busy."

The waiter came by, and we started with charbroiled oysters and bruschetta. Bob seemed ready to start a story, but Raydene jumped in first.

"Tell me how your family is doing," she said.

"We're doing great!" I boasted. "Clayton is excited to start kindergarten, we found a great new preschool for Austen, and we can't wait to meet our little girl coming in the next four months."

Raydene stopped me.

"I don't mean to cut you off, Eric. But that's not what I meant." Raydene had something deeper on her mind.

"Bob shares with me everything he learns at lunch. He talks about how well you intentionally serve our family.

"But with the economy struggling and your livelihood being tied to those outcomes, how is your family doing? This type of pressure can really impact your marriage."

Her words took me by surprise. Raydene cared more about our marriage than their finances.

Angel broke my train of thought with a vulnerable admission.

"It hasn't been easy." She slid her hand over mine and said, "But Eric is focused on the right things. God is taking care of us."

"That's exactly what I wanted to hear," Raydene responded softly, reaching for Bob's hand. "Running a business requires courage."

Casting a knowing glance at her husband, Raydene lightened the mood. "Did Bob tell you I'm responsible for his success?"

"She's my number one investor," Bob chimed in.

Raydene continued, "Bob fell in love with me for my stunning beauty and my money." When she winked at Bob, they were twenty years old again.

"I may come from money, but I did not come from entitlement. Daddy and Momma taught me the value of a dollar and the importance of planning for my future. They blessed me with portions of my inheritance throughout my life so that I could learn how to handle wealth while they were still around as a resource of wisdom.

"Most of my early inheritance was put toward owning companies like Standard Oil, Coca-Cola, and General Motors.

"I told Bob that he would have to marry me for my looks, not my money, because we would live off only his earnings."

Raydene leaned in as if to tell a secret. "Bob never pushed me, but I knew he thought about my inheritance savings when our money was tight. I told him I was waiting for a better investment opportunity.

"Then, in 1990, Bob and Mullins disagreed on project directions. Bob saw opportunities ahead, but Mullins was ready to shut things down.

"I could tell Bob was unsettled, and I finally asked him what was bothering him. He told me how Mullins's fear was casting doubt, but there were two opportunities he couldn't stop thinking about. He didn't have enough money to buy Mullins out and expand.

"When I asked, he said he needed $500,000 for Mullins and another $50,000 for two workover opportunities.

"I reminded him that I had over $750,000 in my inheritance savings and then asked him if he had any collateral to guarantee that he was good for it."

Bob chimed in, "Just my good looks."

Raydene didn't miss a beat: "We transferred the $550,000 from my inheritance account the next day because I knew investing in Bob's courage would pay off!"

"I appreciated her help," Bob began, as Raydene gave him the floor. "But with all that capital invested, I was comforted knowing she still had $200,000 left over.

"I felt optimistic about the future, but Raydene's parents always reminded us to keep some cash on hand for uncertainties."

"Your parents remind me of my grandparents," I said, looking at Raydene.

"They both grew up during the Great Depression and had fruit trees and a garden. They canned vegetables, soups, and jams every season. I still remember canning season and the mason jars stored in the root cellar.

"My grandmother told me, 'Most seasons are good, but we don't have enough food yearly. By canning, we make sure we store enough for the winter and to get us through the years we are short. The most courageous thing you can do is create a margin for the future.'

"Raydene, your inheritance account was like a root cellar for money. You could move forward in courage instead of fear when there was opportunity."

Raydene smiled. "That Depression mindset is just another example of common sense."

"As I think about it, this has relevance today," I said.

"What do you mean?" Raydene asked.

"The markets have been trending downward for two years," I began. "The majority of my conversations with others are rooted in fear.

"We all agree that abundance starts with optimism, but that's been hard to come by lately. While working on my research, I found a ray of hope. When the market falls from a peak, it takes under four years to earn everything back. If that's true, we are more than halfway through this downturn."[5]

"Is it really that quick?" Angel asked.

"That's the average over the last eighty years," I replied.

Bob smiled and looked at Raydene. "Do you see why I like this guy?"

"What is the opportunity?" Bob asked.

"The research reveals two opportunities right now," I began.

"First, we should ensure that we've got two to three years in cash so that you and Raydene have root cellar money until this storm passes."

I looked at Raydene before I revealed the second. "You didn't stop investing in Bob's business, did you?" I asked knowingly.

"Of course not!" she said, grinning. "I made two additional investments when the oil markets were down.

Anytime Bob brought up opportunities during downturns, we knew it was time to act courageously."

"Thank you for confirming our second opportunity," I said triumphantly. "If we are more than halfway through this downturn, let's be courageous while others are fearful and use any extra cash to take advantage of the bargain prices on some great businesses."

Raydene responded, "You two are so similar in the way you think. No wonder you enjoy spending so much time together.

"I see why you trust him to care for our family, Bob." She finished and squeezed his hand.

Something was shifting in the conversation, and I wasn't sure what was happening. I looked at Angel, and she seemed to sense it as well.

Bob responded softly to Raydene, "Eric gives me peace about the future. No matter what happens, I know you and the family will be OK."

"You haven't told them, have you, Bob?" Raydene asked.

"Haven't told us what?" Angel asked kindly.

"The doctor's trips have been a little more than checkups," Bob finally admitted.

His voice broke as he continued, "I've been fighting prostate cancer for the last two years, and it's become more aggressive."

Angel leaned over the table to touch Bob's and Raydene's hands.

I was stunned with a lump in my throat.

"What does that mean, Bob?" I asked, realizing it was a stupid question.

"It means my family is counting on you to take the next chapter in our story. I'll have everything sold and will shut down the office in the next month or so," Bob replied.

Raydene added, "The doctors gave him six months to two years. We know he'll keep fighting until God calls him home."

Bob looked at me, "I've got a favor to ask."

"Anything," I responded, although I could barely speak.

"With the growth of your business, would you mind buying my office furniture so that I have one less thing to worry about?" Bob asked.

I had always admired the big mahogany desk that Bob had sat behind for years.

"I'd be honored," I told Bob.

"Thank you," he replied. "Your friendship means the world to me, Raydene, and the family."

We finished dinner, and despite my efforts, Bob paid the check. Angel and I drove home silently, the weight of Bob's news heavy on our hearts.

Bob and Raydene were some of the most courageous people I knew. I didn't know if we had months or years left together, but I knew Bob's lessons in courage would top anything I had ever learned in a classroom.

THE PRICHARD PRINCIPLE:
PURSUE JOY–BE COURAGEOUS

Fear has a way of creeping into our decisions, especially when times are uncertain. It can paralyze us, keeping us from seeing the opportunities just below the surface. Bob taught me that courage isn't the absence of fear—it's choosing to act in faith despite it. "Fear," he often said, "is just joy in disguise, waiting for us to look deeper." This perspective has helped me reframe how I approach challenges, particularly during tough markets and economic downturns.

Markets will always rise and fall, just like climbing a mountain requires the occasional descent to prepare for the next peak. The key to surviving these dips starts with creating margin. Just like my grandmother canned vegetables to prepare for lean seasons, we help families set aside three to five years of cash reserves. This cushion provides peace of mind, limiting the possibility they would have to sell investments during a downturn.

Thriving, however, requires courage. Downturns can present some of the greatest opportunities to build generational wealth. Over the years, I've developed strategies to deploy excess cash intentionally when markets decline, buying at specific markers and then transitioning back to cash as the market recovers. This isn't about predicting the future—it's about staying grounded in preparation and being ready to act when others are held back by fear. Both of these strategies have become cornerstones of helping families approach uncertainty with courage and common sense. The joy that comes from building a legacy rooted in faith, wisdom, and intention gives us the opportunity not only to survive the valleys but also to set ourselves up to thrive on the next mountaintop.

Know What You Can Control

The old leather chair creaked under Bob's slight frame as he shifted, trying to find a more comfortable position. The man who once filled a room with his booming laugh and larger-than-life presence was now weakening, his body ravaged by cancer. It was mid-July, and the Louisiana summer sun blazed through the window, casting a warm glow on the room. Yet despite the heat outside, there was a chill in the air—an unspoken understanding between two old friends that these moments together were fleeting.

Over the years, our lunches had become a ritual for sharing wisdom, stories, and glasses of wine—a simple pleasure Bob relished and one I had come to associate with my mentor. But those days at the restaurant were a fading memory of the past. His illness made it impossible for him to venture out, so I would visit him at home instead, bringing along a smoothie to help settle his stomach. I could tell the cancer was stalking him and winning. Even so, his mind remained sharp, and his humor, as always, was intact.

"I don't suppose you could find someone to make me a red wine smoothie?" Bob inquired one afternoon, a twinkle in his eye.

I chuckled, but there was a heaviness in my heart. Watching the once-strong oilman deteriorate was difficult, especially knowing how vibrant he had once been. Darcy and Raydene were doing their best to care for him, but no amount of compassion, back rubs, or visits from the grandkids could keep the cancer from progressing. Yet, through it all, Bob never lost control of the one thing that truly mattered: his attitude.

Not knowing how many visits we had left, I sat by his side as my thoughts closed in on me. Angel and I were facing our own battle. Our newborn daughter, Gracyn, had been whisked off to the neonatal intensive care unit just after her birth a week prior, unable to breathe on her own. It was the kind of situation that shakes a parent to their core, and the fear that we might lose her weighed heavily on my mind.

"How's Gracyn doing?" Bob asked, his voice weak.

"She's fighting," I replied, trying to keep my voice steady. "But the doctors say we're not out of the woods yet."

Bob nodded slowly. "We don't know how this will turn out," he said. "But I can tell you from all my years that the only thing we can control in these situations is our attitude."

Silence came and stood with me as I looked at my friend. It lingered until Bob pushed it away, his voice tinged with the wisdom of a man who had seen more than most.

"Did I ever tell you about how Raydene and I survived the death of our son?"

I shook my head, surprised that this story had never come up in all our years of conversation.

"It was after I'd split from Mullins. The kids were out of the house.

"Our Scott was in a car wreck, and he left behind his wife and two daughters."

It was as if silence reached out and steadied Bob's emotions.

"That year was the hardest of my life."

His eyes glazed with the memory. "We were all in shock. We didn't get much done.

"We just got out of bed every morning and put one foot in front of the other. I carried a heavy load. I had to keep everyone moving forward."

He paused, the memory weighing on him, even after fifteen years. "I spent a lot of time praying that year.

"I asked God, 'Why not take me instead?' I argued with Him about why He would leave a widow and her children like that.

"Through my grief, I discovered something."

Bob was showing more strength than I had seen in months as he grabbed my hands, looked me in the eye, and shared, "My attitude controls my outcome!"

Bob's words hung as I navigated my fears and uncertainties.

"I tried to find something to be grateful for daily," he started. "The first day, it was the sunrise. The next, it was a warm cup of coffee."

He thought for a moment then continued, "In time, I prioritized gratitude at the beginning of every day."

He paused, and I handed him his foam cup of water.

I interrupted him: "Bob, we can discuss this later."

"Eric, I don't know if I *have* later."

He continued, "Each day built on the next, and my attitude of gratitude began to rub off on the family.

"In my darkest moment, I learned to look at what I can control and to keep my attitude focused on that.

"What are the positive things you can focus on?" he asked.

I took a deep breath, my eyes looking up as I began to think. "Angel. She is a wonderful and supportive wife," I began.

Bob nodded, inviting silence to force me to keep going.

"Clayton and Austen are growing up strong and healthy.

"Dr. Clancy and her team love Gracyn and are giving us hope.

"Darcy and other friends are helping with the boys so we can visit the hospital.

"And I have a thriving business, not to mention friends, like this old oilman I know. I think his name is Prichard. You ever met him?"

The old oilman smiled softly, pleased with my response.

"Speaking of business," he said, his voice gaining a bit of strength, "Can we talk about something on my mind?"

"Of course," I responded, wondering how much more energy he had.

"Raydene and I have been blessed, and before I go home to be with God, I want to use our abundance to help others," Bob said.

"Like The University of Oklahoma?" I asked, trying to keep the mood light while looking at the crimson and cream blanket covering his legs.

"'Boomer Sooner!'" Bob exclaimed as strongly as he could muster.

I chuckled, enjoying the welcome distraction.

"What are you thinking?" I asked.

"Two things are weighing heavily," my mentor replied. His voice was growing steadier, almost as if the conversation had given him a second wind.

"First, we want to help Basin Bridge Christian Church's Grief Share ministry. They help families through the pain of losing a loved one, just like we experienced with Scott's passing."

He swallowed hard, took a sip of water, then continued.

"Second, we want to establish an endowment for the Magnolia Hospital Cancer Center. This disease is a physical and financial drain. We want to help ease that burden for families struggling to cover the costs."

With that, he sat back in the chair, and I knew he had given all he had for the day.

"I will make sure those get done," I promised.

"I know you will," Bob said with that old familiar twinkle in his eye.

"I've got one more request," he said, with a hint of his mischievous nature.

"Why don't you bring me a red wine smoothie next time? This chocolate just isn't the same."

I left shortly thereafter and hugged Raydene and Darcy as I walked out the door.

Within a few days, Gracyn began to turn the corner.

By mid-August, Angel and I could finally bring Gracyn home to the nursery decked out in pink, green, and lace.

My old friend's encouragement became a way of life. Each morning started with a simple prayer: "God, thank You for . . ."

I could control my attitude, focusing on abundance and intending to influence my family and business the way Bob influenced me.

I visited my friend several more times, and although I never found a red wine smoothie, we finished setting up the gifts to the church and hospital.

In early November, my phone rang. It was Raydene.

"Eric, my old oilman is gone."

We cried together, and after the call, I took the rest of the afternoon off.

It was hard to believe Bob was gone.

But I knew I could look back with gratitude on the lessons he taught me and his profound impact on my life. Bob's death left a void, but it also created a legacy—a reminder that no matter what life throws our way, our attitude is one thing we can control. And in that control lies the power to shape our outcomes and turn challenges into opportunities.

THE PRICHARD PRINCIPLE: PURSUE JOY—HAVE AN ATTITUDE OF GRATITUDE

Life is full of things we can't control, but one thing we always have power over is our attitude. Bob taught me that our mindset shapes how we navigate challenges and embrace opportunities. His wisdom still echoes in my daily life, especially on hard days. "Gratitude," he said, "is the key to shifting your perspective and focusing on what truly matters."

In our home, this principle has become a family tradition. Each morning at breakfast, we take a moment to share something we're grateful for and a prayer request for the day. It's simple, but it keeps us grounded, focused on God's blessings, and connected to each other. That daily reminder of gratitude has transformed how we approach the ups and downs of life.

In my work, I've also adopted this principle with the families we serve. When markets or the economy is down, it's easy to get caught up in fear. But gratitude shifts our focus to what we can control. We use these downturns as opportunities—managing tax liabilities or reinvesting for the future. When markets are up, we look for ways to give back, like making charitable gifts from investments instead of cash. It's incredible to watch families discover how gratitude not only preserves their wealth but also creates generational blessings through generosity.

Return on Intention

It's been over twenty years since I interrupted Bob's lunch and he first said, "Why don't you sit down." I had no idea how that small moment would impact and influence the rest of my life. One of my most treasured possessions is now the large mahogany desk in my office that Bob once sat behind. Every day, I think about Bob. Writing this book felt like the old oilman was right here in the room with me. His voice, easy laugh, and the smell of Cabernet became almost tangible as I recounted the lessons I learned from Bob.

It's hard to capture and summarize all the characteristics of this remarkable man. Still, in a world that values financial return on investment, Bob was a man who flipped the script and valued *return on intention*. Put simply, Bob recognized that true wealth is made up of relationships, common sense, and joy.

To this day, I'm still amazed at how a simple lunch invitation blossomed into such a deep and meaningful friendship. Bob understood the value of investing in relationships. I saw it in the way he cherished Raydene, Darcy, and the rest of his family. He was fully present whenever he was with them—intentionally engaged in every moment. But it wasn't just his family. Bob made it a priority to connect deeply with everyone he encountered. He knew the waiters and waitresses at The Bistro by name, and he cared about their stories—their families, their dreams, and their prayers.

Bob recognized that relationships matter, and he had a gift for helping others see their potential. My mentor showed me that the most profound gift you can give someone is to love them enough to help them uncover the possibilities they couldn't see for themselves. Today, this lesson shapes one of my greatest pursuits: intentionally building relationships. When I focus on building relationships, the *return on intention* grows exponentially.

Bob also had a rare gift for seeing the world through a lens of common sense and simplicity. His wisdom was a beacon of clarity in an age overwhelmed by information. The more I have lived, the more I have realized that what was common sense for Bob and other members of the Greatest Generation is not so common anymore. I've come to see it as uncommon sense. That's what Bob taught me. While many people complicate things to sound intelligent, my friend had a way of stripping everything down to its essentials. His straightforward approach was refreshing, especially in a world in which clarity is often sacrificed for complexity.

In finance, notorious for its layers of intricacy, Bob taught me how to tune out the noise. Rather than chasing every new tool or strategy, he focused on four guiding principles: Be an owner, seize opportunities, recognize erosion, and, most importantly, avoid *di-worse-ification*. Bob's perspective stood in stark contrast to the distractions of Wall Street and the media, and his ideas offer a grounded and simple path to financial success.

Bob's influence wasn't just limited to finance; his faith had a profound impact on my spiritual life as well. He understood that faith is about cultivating a personal relationship with the Creator of the universe. While many people look to preachers, podcasts, and books to define their beliefs, Bob embodied the importance of going directly to the source—reading the Bible and praying daily. I've now developed a daily habit of studying Scripture and praying over my day, which has deepened my connection with God. It's not complex, but it's powerful. This habit, rooted in the uncommonsense wisdom my mentor lived by, has created an exponential *return on intention* in my life.

The greatest gift Bob left me was the ability to find joy in every moment. For him, joy often began with a good meal and a glass of wine, but that was just the start. Bob taught me the power of embracing joy and gratitude, no matter the circumstances.

Running my business has demanded courageous decisions, especially when investing in future growth during economic downturns. You might say owning a business in the financial services industry is not for the faint of heart. But in the difficult moments, when I focus on the joy of my family or find peace on a long run through the trails of my Northshore neighborhood, I discover that courage naturally follows. Gratitude forces me to recognize my own abundance. Bob, the wise oilman, helped me see that when we align with God's purpose and let go of our ego, we experience His provision. This is something Bob did effortlessly.

Bob's pursuit of a different kind of ROI—*return on intention*—defines a life well lived. Focusing on relationships, uncommon sense, and joy each day is the path to peace in a world consumed by distractions and fear.

With five simple words, Bob forever changed my life. I now use them as often as I can: "Lunch is always on me."

Afterword

Bob's legacy continues to guide me every day. Each morning as I sit behind his old mahogany desk, I'm reminded of the wisdom he shared and the life he lived. Bob was more than just an oilman from the Greatest Generation—he was a mentor, a friend, and a man of deep principles. The lessons he left behind have become the foundation of how my company serves families, helping them build legacies of their own.

The Prichard Principles are more than just ideas; they're a road map for intentionally pursuing joy, celebrating relationships, and applying common sense. My prayer is that these principles will inspire you, as they have inspired me, to create a legacy of abundance and impact that will bless your family for generations to come.

THE PRICHARD PRINCIPLES

CELEBRATE RELATIONSHIPS

- *Return on Intention* Trumps Return on Investment (chapter 1)
- Family Is Your Top Asset (chapter 2)

USE COMMON SENSE

- Think Like an Owner (chapter 4)
- Avoid Erosion (chapter 5)
- Avoid *Di-worse-ification* (chapter 6)
- Use Research to Reveal Opportunities (chapter 7)

PURSUE JOY

- Abundance Defeats Scarcity (chapter 3)
- Be Courageous (chapter 8)
- Have an Attitude of Gratitude (chapter 9)

If you enjoyed this book, and you'd like resources to help apply the practical wisdom to your situation, your family, or your team; you'll love what we've put together at www.linktr.ee/BistroBook

Endnotes

1. Vitali Alexeev and Francis Tapon, "Equity Portfolio Diversification: How Many Stocks Are Enough? Evidence from Five Developed Markets," *Financial Research Network Research Paper Series* (November 29, 2012), https://dx.doi.org/10.2139/ssrn.2182295.

2. Hosea 4:6.

3. Inflation data sourced from J.P.Morgan's *Guide to the Markets* as of April 30, 2024, accessed at https://am.jpmorgan.com/us/en/asset-management/adv/insights/market-insights/guide-to-the-markets/.

4. Robert Carey, "Concerned About Keeping Pace with Inflation?," *Market Commentary Blog*, First Trust Portfolios, April 25, 2024, https://www.ftportfolios.com/Commentary/MarketCommentary/2024/4/25/concerned-about-keeping-pace-with-inflation.

5. Mark Hulbert, "Bear Markets Can Be Shorter Than You Think," MarketWatch, March 21, 2016, https://www.marketwatch.com/story/bear-markets-can-be-shorter-than-you-think-2016-03-21.